Survival Guide for the Skint

how to feel richer

on your present income

Jackie Wilkinson

i

Paperback ISBN 1904312802   ISBN 13 9781904312802
Published in the UK and USA by MX Publishing
335 Princess Park Manor, Royal Drive,
London, N11 3GX
www.mxpublishing.co.uk

Cartoon illustrations © Colin Shelbourn, www.shelbourn.com

Cover compilation and colour design by www.staunch.com

This book is dedicated to

all my friends and colleagues

whose constant bemoaning of

money shortages

inspired me to write

this survival guide.

CONTENTS

ACKNOWLEDGEMENTS

As well as my own experience, this book benefits from the knowledge and experience of the Sally Thompson, Alan Neal, Mollie Hirst, Mike Hirst and Maurice Hirst. Sarah Hutton, Kirsty Skivington and Cait Moore helped particularly with the chapter on children. I would like to thank everyone for their ideas and input.

I valued the skills of Maurice Hirst, Nick Hance, Sally Thompson and Hilary Templar who proof read the manuscript. In spite of my best efforts, I have not been able to find sources for all quotes.

Thanks to the West Cumberland hospital for the polystyrene box like the one I used to sit on and to David Mart for taking a picture of me sitting on it.

Colin Shelbourn took on the important task of illustrator and captured wonderfully my vision of the cliff-top path and its perils as an analogy to our journey through life.

Thanks to Steve Emecz who showed his faith in this book by taking it on.

Finally, thanks to my beloved husband Garry, for allowing me to write a second book after experiencing the first one.

PREFACE

My husband and I sat side by side on the steps that linked the dining room to the spacious lounge below. It was twilight. There were no curtains yet at the large windows, no furniture, just us newly moved into our dream house.

The day we had become a couple we had also sat on the floor. Then I had no furniture because I couldn't afford any. No table, no fridge, no bed. Just a polystyrene packing box to sit on.

I used to say I would have made it if I could turn on the tap and have hot water whenever I wanted. So I was already content even then, clearly skint, but surviving.

You may be thinking that this is a book about being skint but it isn't. It's a book about stopping being skint.

I am not a financial expert. I won't baffle you with "accountant-speak". I'm a survivor and I'll share with you some simple ideas that have worked for me and for others. Here's to your survival.

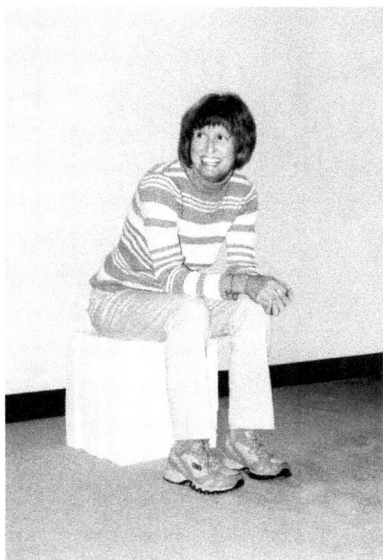

(Photo by David Mart)

1 INTRODUCTION

It's a tough world. When you're negotiating your way along the cliff-top path of life, there are high lifestyle expectations and the perils of insecure jobs. Predators lie in wait to devour you and Sirens[1] sing to lure you to your ruin.

Are you walking along confident and secure in your good management of your money? Or are you living on the ragged edge, teetering on the brink, juggling bills, loans and credit cards while the desire to have all the bright, shiny things constantly thrust at you threatens to upset your balance? Everyone wants your money and they don't care if you end up broken on the rocks of financial disaster.

---

1   In Greek myths, Sirens were savage creatures that sang a sweet song to lure sailors onto their island. Then they devoured them!

The financial workings of the world are increasingly interconnected and unstable. One wobble in confidence, some media hype or a bit of mismanagement in one country can lead to a global financial catastrophe[2]. To survive you need to be prepared, alert and ready to defend yourself.

Skint or Rich?

Before getting down to the nitty-gritty of financial survival, what do I mean by "rich"?

I've noticed that people plead poverty regardless of how much they earn. It's the reason I decided to write this book. No-one seems to be satisfied!

As students, we were all poor; we were supposed to be. But I coped OK, avoiding the large debts that friends suffered. After

---

2   As was so dramatically demonstrated in 2008.

graduating, I got a job with low pay. I managed while others on similar wages struggled. When I moved to a better job, things were easier. Later on I came across people earning large salaries who should have felt rich, but amazingly they still moaned about being skint.

Your own view of money will change as your life's circumstances change. I used to feel flush if I could take a bus instead of walking, weighed down with my weekly shopping. Now I have a car which is just as well because I'm not so young and wouldn't make the four mile walk back up the hill from town, carrying half a dozen supermarket bags.

So what is 'rich'? I had thought it depended on how much money you earned but it doesn't seem to be like that. I know people who have had huge amounts of money coming in.

Unfortunately they spent even huger amounts and stayed skint. Some ended up losing everything.

Clearly, then, "rich" is not something that can be defined in absolute terms (i.e. £x = rich). "Rich" is a relative quantity. For example:

Mr Smith earns £500 per week and spends £450 a week on mortgage, bills etc. leaving £50 a week spending money.

Miss Brown earns £250 per week and spends £150 a week on bills leaving £100 a week to spend.

Which of them feels richer? - Miss Brown!

So you'll feel richer if you live within your means rather than at the limit of your means. (Continually living beyond your means leads to debt or even bankruptcy.) It's very interesting that Mr Smith, who earned more, ended up with so little money to play with.

Satisfaction

The problem can be rooted in a mismatch between our expectations and our reality. Contentment comes from living in a way that matches your situation. Frustration sets in when your reality is different from your vision. You probably know people who have more money than you as well as some who have less. All of them have their own joys and concerns.

> Having enough money to live on is not about having lots of it but knowing that you can manage without very much of it.
> Jonathan Atkinson[3]

---

3   Building Self-Esteem, A Practical Guide to Growing in Confidence, Sue Atkinson, 2001, Lion Hudson Plc.

People in Britain have more things and more wealth than ever before. Are we happier? No. We just have more stuff to look after and end up going to car boot sales to get rid of it. Talk to your grandparents. Research shows that we are now 4 times better off than we were 40 years ago but this has had no effect on our overall happiness[4].

Happiness is founded on relationships, not possessions. If you live a life based on things, your thirst for more will never be satisfied however much you have. More is not always better as the rich and famous have discovered in their affluent but sometimes empty lives.

So what <u>can</u> money do? Money can give you a home, security, freedom to live the way you want, the means to provide for your kids, engage in sports and hobbies, or to travel.

4   Family Circle magazine circa 2002 (sadly no longer published).

It's also painfully true that lack of money can leave you cold, hungry, stressed and miserable. *Survival Guide for the Skint* tackles the causes and considers the solutions.

Survival Guide for the Skint

As you go through this book we'll find out where your money goes (you might be surprised) and how you can hang onto more of it. We'll tackle the dangers you'll face and find ways for you to protect yourself. You'll also decide where you want to get to in life and create your own map of how to get there.

Going back to basics, we'll look at life's priorities and you'll consider what's really important to you. There's a lot on shopping (chapter 6) and children (chapter 9) where your money can go with alarming speed. Major outlays, the place you live and transport, have their own chapter (The Big Ones, chapter 7). Money management is dealt with of course, in chapters on cash, credit and saving (chapters 4, 8 and 5).

You might not have expected sections on slimming or being environmentally friendly (chapters 12 and 10) but they too contain ideas for saving money.

In the end, you'll be able to walk the path along the cliff-top, secure in the knowledge that you can survive.

2 AWARENESS - the big eye opener

Life isn't easy when you're skint. There are so many problems and everything is so complicated. Where will you start? How can you sort it all out and get back in control? Many of us are ignorant of how money works and some are plain scared of it. We avoid thinking about it too much but if you walk near the edge of a cliff without looking where you're going, sooner or later you'll fall off.

A key part of survival is knowing where you are. If you're in the dark, it's time to put on a head-torch, open your eyes wide and have a look around.

Put yourself on the map
The thing with money is that you need to understand where it all goes.....

Knowledge is power. If you can clearly identify a problem, you've taken a big step towards solving it. (This is true in many areas of life, not just money.) The first step is to spend a little time working out your finances on paper or your computer screen. You're going to create a map, starting by finding out where you are now.

To work out what you spend, use the following table (Table 1) as a starting point. I used my bank statement to create this list. I haven't included things that usually come off your pay before you get it (e.g. tax, National Insurance and pension payments). You can add in anything else you think of and delete items that don't apply to you.

Include the total costs for your household. You'll have bills to tell you exactly how much some things are (e.g. council tax) and others will vary (e.g. fuel bills).[5]

Lots of things have to be paid monthly so, to keep it simple, put everything in monthly equivalents. If you have some costs that are paid only once a year, divide them by 12. Other bills, like water rates, come twice a

---

5   If you find you have difficulty keeping track of all your bills and paperwork, you might like to try reading Taming the Paper Tiger by Barbara Hemphill.

year; divide these by 6. Estimate as accurately as you can.

Remember to include things you get on credit; you still have to pay for them (contrary to popular belief!). You may notice that I haven't put credit card bills on the list. Credit cards are not things that you buy but a method of paying for things that you buy, just like cash and cheques. So if you use yours in the supermarket each week, the amount should appear next to food on the list.

On the other hand, I have included an item for interest payments. If you owe money on your cards, you'll have to pay interest even if you don't buy anything. (You want to have something to show for every penny you spend; don't worry, we'll work on reducing interest payments in chapter 8.) Here you go:

Table 1 - Outgoings

Item	Monthly equivalent
Mortgage / Rent	
Endowment (or life assurance for mortgage)	
Home Insurance (building)	
Home Insurance (contents)	
Electricity/Gas/Oil/Solid fuel	
Water Rates	
Council Tax	
Telephone (including landline, mobile, computer dial up/Broadband)	
Pension payments (if you pay into a pension separately from your employment)	
Home maintenance, decorating and repairs	
Support payments for children not living with you	
Interest payments on loans and cards	

Food (main weekly groceries x $4^1/_3$)

Food (incidentals like sandwiches, coffees and chocolate)

Toiletries, cosmetics and hair products

Household cleaning products

Clothes

Train/bus fares

Medical/dental/optician

Regular savings

Sports/hobbies

Car or motorbike   - tax

                   - insurance

                   - servicing, repairs and tyres

                   - fuel (petrol/diesel)

                    - depreciation/saving for next one

Newspapers and magazines

Entertainment (eating out, cinema, alcohol, DVDs, music downloads, computer games, gambling etc)

Cigarettes/tobacco	
Holidays	
Pets - food	
- insurance	
- bedding	
- Vets' bills	
Gifts and cards - birthdays	
Gifts and cards - Christmas	
Giving to charities	

The first thing that struck me is how long the list is! It's no wonder the money goes so fast. There are so many things to pay for, how can any of us manage to live at all?

It can be done. So, now take a deep breath and add it all up to get the ...

Total outgoings (monthly)	

Next work out your income. Include wages, benefits and other income.

You did your outgoings in monthly equivalents so we'll do income the same way. If you're paid weekly, put in $4^1/_3$ times your weekly pay.

Interest on savings is calculated daily but you may only be notified annually so use this amount divided by 12.

Again add and delete items so that the list is right for you.

Table 2 - Income

Source	Monthly equivalent
Wages (net pay after tax, National Insurance and pension payments)	
Pension	
Benefits	
Allowances	
Child support payments	
Interest on savings	
Share dividends	

Total income (monthly)	

Finally, compare the two totals.

If the total of your outgoings is more than your income, you have a problem. You're heading for the rocks of financial ruin at the bottom of the cliff. This is a bad place to be. The rest of this book will help you climb back up. In extreme survival situations you need a guide, so get professional help as well (see chapter 8 which looks at debt and the Resources section). Don't try to go it alone.

If your outgoings are only slightly less than your income, you'll often feel short of money for the things you need and want. You're walking close to the edge and will benefit from gaining more control.

If your total outgoings are currently less than your income, you'll be able to relax as you walk along the cliff top-path. The question to ask yourself is how you would mange if life's circumstances gave you a knock. Would you hang on, or would you fall off? There may be things that you could do to make yourself more secure.

Explore the territory

That was the theory but does it match your reality? How well do you really understand your spending?

When I first did this exercise myself, I didn't feel the result was right. I should have had some money to spare but I didn't. Where had the rest of it gone? What had I under estimated?

I started to carry a pen and a bit of cardboard with me and wrote down every penny I parted with, right down to the last bar of chocolate. Each week I added up my spending grouped under some of the headings from the list in Table 1 - Outgoings. Try this and see what result you get. It will reveal your spending weaknesses. I was amazed to find that the real pattern of my spending wasn't the same as I thought it would be. You'll turn up some surprises too.

Keep an <u>honest</u> record of **every** penny you spend for a month. Don't miss a thing, however small. The more you can learn about where your money goes, the better your chances of preventing the pounds slipping through your fingers.

Just knowing what your habits are will change them. It's a bit like keeping a record of everything you eat when you're trying to lose weight. You'll change what you eat automatically, just by learning more about what you really are eating.

Some examples of common unrecognised or underestimated spending weaknesses are:

- Incidental food (chocolate, coffees, snacks)
- Magazines
- CDs
- Cigarettes
- Alcohol
- Clothes
- Toiletries/Cosmetics
- Mobile 'phone
- "Collectables"

Tip the balance in your favour

Look more closely at each of the items in Table 1, your list of outgoings. Which can you reduce? Anything that you pay for regularly is an ideal target for saving.   Even if the amounts appear small they add up quickly. My own discovery was the surprisingly large amount of money I was spending on drinks and snacks. Look at your household bills too. Shopping around for the best deals on mortgages, insurance, energy provider and telephone services can save a lot.   There are internet sites to help you compare and decide.

Check your income too.   Make sure that you're claiming all the benefits and allowances that you're entitled to[6].

Where do you want to get to?

We needed to look at the reality of your situation to get a grip of it but in our culture we're actually a bit too good at focussing on problems.   We think about problems, talk about problems, worry about problems, moan

---

6   www.direct.gov.uk

and complain about problems. If you want things to change for the better, you need to practice thinking about what you <u>do</u> want and talking about the things in life that are already good. If you can describe how you really want life to be, you have taken another huge step towards making it come true. Take a tip from sports coaching and ruthlessly think, talk about and notice only what you and other people do right.

We use maps to help us find our way to places. So where do you want to go? We all have different hopes and dreams. It's important before starting to reach for your vision to make sure that it's truly your own. We're bombarded by so much advertising that we can get sucked in to wanting the exotic goodies and glamorous lifestyles they pressure us to desire. But do we really want them?

We think winning the lottery would make us happy. It isn't true. Incredibly, research shows that after a year, people are equally happy whether they had suffered an accident causing paralysis or were lottery winners. Harvard psychologist Dan Gilbert says this is because your brain can 'synthesize' happiness.[7] Your circumstances have less effect than you'd expect.

I have heard it said that the more you have to live for, the less you need to live on. Being happy is not always to do with the things you own. It's about family, friendships, quality of life, freedom of choice and the ability to enjoy what you do have. Only you know what's right for you. Spend some time thinking about what you want from life.

7
http://articles.mercola.com/sites/articles/archive/2007/10/30/the-secret-of-how-to-be-happy.aspx Text and a video of Dan Gilbert explaining his findings.

This book aims to help people who want to better manage their money. But perhaps you enjoy the excitement of being wild and irresponsible yet fear growing old and dull. Rather than changing your lifestyle to survive, you may think it's so important to fly high today that you're prepared to crash and burn tomorrow. It's your life. What you choose to do with it is your responsibility, as are your resulting joys, catastrophes and adventures.

Do the people you live with have similar aspirations to you or do they want something different? Talk about it with friends and family. Invest in a coach and get some clarity for your goal. The more vividly you can describe where you want to end up, the better. Write it down. Draw pictures. Tell other people. Imagine it. If you're keen to get stuck in straight away, you could have hit on the right vision for you. The more you think about your desired destination, the more likely you are to get there. Focus on solutions, successes and blessings.

If you don't believe that this can make a real difference, then you haven't tried it before. You can throw yourself into positive thinking - it's free!

Finding your way

You may be perched precariously on the cliff edge or perhaps you're clinging to the rock face part way down. You don't want to be skint any more but the thought of working out a budget or starting to save may fill you with dread. It's down to you to save yourself. Even if it isn't your fault that you ended up here, no one else will bail you out. There isn't a fairy Godmother with a magic wand. No knight on a white charger will ride up to your door. But you can survive.

Motivate yourself to action. Some people think in terms of moving towards all the things they want; others like to move away from difficulties. Learn what it is that gets you going. You need to work as a team with your nearest and dearest. Some of the changes you might have to make won't be easy so you'll all have to pull together. This is what survival is about.

On your map you now know where you are and where you want to end up. If the two are poles apart, you won't be able to make the change overnight. If you try to do too much all at once you might give up. Break your journey into steps that you know you can manage. This will keep you motivated as you succeed in making progress.

We tend to look at life from where we are now, gazing into the future, like looking down a street. Imagine that you went to the other end of the street, to your future, say ten years from now. Look back the other way towards the present. Does it look different? From there you can see the consequences of your actions along the way and how they shape the life you will have. Doing this exercise will give you a new perspective of the journey and some of the steps along the way.

Once you can see clearly, you can avoid walking off the edge of the cliff. When you understand what's happening, you can take control. You don't have to make the same mistakes as other people to learn the right lessons. As Alvin Hall's grandmother Rosa Lee advised him, you just need to watch and listen.[8]

---

8   Money for Life, Alvin Hall, Hodder and Stoughton, 2000.

So find out what successful people do and do the same things until you get the same results.[9] Other people have survived being skint. I did and so can you.

Every time you take a step along the path, get excited and congratulate yourself. You're becoming a survivor.

9   Eat that Frog, Brian Tracy, Berrett-Koehler Publishers Inc, 2002.

3 PRIORITIES

In chapter 2 we found out where your money goes. The list of demands on your purse is very long. You may not always have enough money for everything so it helps to be clear about which things really matter.

You're on the expedition of life, out in the wilds and you need the essentials of life to survive. So what are they?

Maslow's[10] Hierarchy of Needs

Self actualisation	Reaching your potential
Esteem needs	Self respect, confidence
Social needs	Belonging, love, friendship
Safety needs	**Physical and emotional security**
Physiological needs	**Warmth, shelter, sleep, food, water**

---

10   Abraham Maslow 1908-1970, professor of psychology, New York. Developed the 'hierarchy of needs' model of human motivation.

Human beings have a few basic needs (at the bottom of the table) and a huge range of higher needs and desires. If your basic needs are not met, then your higher desires become irrelevant. If you're homeless and starving the good grades you got at school will not seem important. The trouble of course, is that as your lower needs are satisfied, your wants escalate. The priority for your budget is to make sure that you're fed, housed and warm.

Priorities for your budget
Food - Man may not live by bread alone but you cannot survive for long without food - budget for it.

What you eat also has a large impact on your state of health and your mood. Have a look at the contents of your supermarket trolley and decide whether they will keep your wallet and your body in good shape.   There's more on food in chapter 6, Shopping.

Mortgage/rent - You must pay or you could lose your home.

Take care if you're thinking of moving house and increasing your mortgage.   Someone will always be willing to lend you more than you can safely borrow.   The interest rates can do weird and not very wonderful things so leave a comfort zone.   If the rates go up, you'll cope if you planned for it.   If the rates go down, you'll have money to spare which you can spend or save.   See chapter 7, The Big Ones for more on homes.

Clothes - Society and the great British weather dictate that we must be clad.   There's a limit to what you need and a wardrobe stuffed full of clothes will not help you in your fight for survival. There's a section on clothes in chapter 6, Shopping. Make sure you set aside enough money for clothes to protect your body and to make you look good.

Clothes are an especially important budget item for children because they grow so fast. Everyone loves to give baby clothes to expectant mums - but most of them will never be worn because they will very quickly be outgrown. See chapter 9, Children.

Bills - When you go to the shops, you have to pay on the spot. Services like water, electricity, gas, the telephone etc. you use in advance of payment. Make sure you pay the bills when they do arrive. If you don't, your service providers are entitled to cut you off.

Mobility - Transport is important for most people and is essential for the freedom and independence of those people who cannot walk or who have physical disabilities. In today's world, life becomes a lot easier if you can get around. Whether you drive a car, cycle or take the bus, transport costs money and must be budgeted for in accordance with how important it is for you. Using transport to go to work, visit family, take part in sport or social activities also meets the need that Maslow identified for 'belonging'.

Perspective

I know people who have a great deal of money and others who have hardly any. They live in different sorts of houses and have different holidays but their levels of happiness are the same. Channel 4[11] ran a series in which rich business people went undercover in needy areas before giving away some of their money to support good projects. Some of the

---

11   Channel 4 TV, The Secret Millionaire.

participants expected to struggle without all their usual trappings and luxuries but were surprised to find that they had a wonderful time.

In Thailand, a traveller called Genki met a family living in ply-board and metal huts, very poor compared to most people in Britain, but healthy and happy[12]. Without TV, magazines and the internet to tell them that they might lack anything, they enjoyed life, each other and what they had.

There are still millions of people around the world living in real poverty without enough food each day to satisfy their hunger or clean water to drink. They die of starvation and disease in their tens of thousands every day. Peter Singer[13] has written about their plight

---

12   Genki, As posted on www.mercola.com in response to an article on happiness.
13   The Life You Can Save, Peter Singer, Picador, 2009.

and how giving even a little can bring change. Giving connects us to the world's needy. It helps us to keep a sense of perspective on what life's about and what really matters.

4 CASH - your ultimate survival tool

Cash was the secret of my survival as a student and early in my working life when I had hardly any money to live on. If drastic measures are called for, cash makes a brilliant barrier to stop you falling off the cliff.

At university I paid my rent up front, put aside money for my fare home and worked out a weekly budget. Every Friday evening I withdrew that amount of cash. On Saturday morning I bought food for the week. I had to live on what was left until the following Friday. When the cash ran out I stopped spending. Foolproof. Running out of money wasn't pleasant; no more beer or chocolate is serious for a student. But it had to be done and after four years I came away with my degree but no debt. (I recognise that student loans are now almost inevitable but using these principles, you can minimise your debt.)

In chapter 2 we worked out how much money you have available to live on. It's very important to get this bit right if you're living close to the edge. Arrange for regular payment of bills where you can. Then set a weekly limit for spending that covers food, clothes, petrol/bus fares etc. Get the money out on the same day each week. Buy the food first because you can't live without eating.

Why buy food first?
A friend of mine used a similar cash scheme. One day we were working together and his stomach was rumbling. I asked if he was hungry. He was; he had run out of food. It was still 2 days until he went to get more cash and the only thing left in his cupboard was a packet of cornflakes which he'd been eating since Tuesday! Crazy. I had food so I cooked his lunch.

With what's left buy other priority items next (see chapter 3, Priorities) and leave until last any things you don't need but only want. When the money for a week has run out, stop spending – it's that simple.

When you shop with cash, you'll discover it's much harder to hand over a wad of crisp notes than a bit of plastic. And when your pocket is empty you have to stop, so you can't blow your budget. With plastic it's hard to remember after the first few transactions how much you have already spent and to keep track of how much is left.

This may sound ridiculously simple but using cash is actually a very powerful way of staying in control.

Are you living close to the edge? Use cash.

5 SAVINGS - your life line

If your income and your outgoings are finely balanced, what will you do for money when something unexpected comes up? Life's fortunes can go either way with alarming speed. Bad luck happens. It's a question of when, not if. Savings are like an emergency safety rope for your security and protection against painful falls. They're a lifeline to save you.

My first job was poorly paid so I didn't have much more money coming in than when I was a student. Also my expenses were greater so I was worse off. I managed by living to the same principles as before.

I shared a house with some nurses who spent all their weekly pay, often before the end of the week. When one of them was faced with a family problem, she couldn't afford the bus fare to go and visit her Mum. I suggested that she raid her savings since it was an emergency. She didn't have any, none at all. I couldn't believe it.

More astounding still, later I met people with successful careers and really big salaries who were in exactly the same situation. They just spent more to match or exceed their income. People are falling over themselves to get rid of the money they break their backs to earn. Surely you deserve not to be skint after you've worked so hard?

Buck the trend; start saving
Start thinking of saving as something you will do as a matter of routine rather than a vague concept you'll get round to if you have any cash left over. (If you have any debt it's also important to read chapter 8.) Aristotle said,

'We are what we repeatedly do. Excellence then is not an act but a habit.'[14] Saving is a good habit.

It's easiest to save by setting up a direct debit to a savings account with the payment date just after your income arrives in the bank. That way you'll hardly notice that you're putting money away. You'll very quickly get used to living on the reduced amount you have to spend each month. Meanwhile your savings will grow and grow.

If you have never saved before, be kind to yourself and start small. Develop a routine as soon as you can. Get into the habit of putting part of your income straight into your savings. Even when I had a paper round as a child, I used to go to the post office next door to the newsagent and buy savings stamps with most

---

14   Aristotle 384-322BC.

45

of my wages. If you get a pay rise, try saving the extra money. You'll never notice because it's money you haven't had before.

Save consistently and you'll be surprised how it adds up, especially when you get interest. Get some emergency funds behind you and put yourself in a position of control, power and choice.

Can you wait?
It's human nature to appreciate things in direct proportion to our investment. That is, the price we pay for them, whether in money, time or effort.

Athletes who have to struggle for years to achieve their first gold medal appreciate that success more. The challenges they experience along the way are essential to growth and make winning taste sweeter.

People who build up businesses from small beginnings or who start at the bottom and climb the ladder to senior positions in a company, have a great sense of achievement.

If you stroll in and buy a car on a loan or finance agreement, the pain of keeping up the payments will continue long after the shine has gone off the paintwork. If you save up to buy a car, there's a real thrill when you drive away and know it's all yours. Even if it's a bit of an old wreck, as some of mine were, you'll love that car and enjoy it.

What will you save for?

There will have been times in your life when it would have helped you to have some savings available. What sort of things might you benefit from saving for in future? Here are a few examples. There will be lots others you can think of.

Emergencies. Aim to build up a few months' income, not to be used except in a crisis.

Holidays. It's bad enough leaving paradise to come home without having a huge credit card bill waiting for you on the mat.

Cars. Start saving for your next one the day after you bought the last one. You may even get a discount for a cash sale instead of paying over the odds on finance (see chapter 7).

Old age. It's never too early to start paying into a pension.

Manage your accounts

Current accounts are for using. Money can come in and go out often. These are the workhorse accounts that help you channel your money where it needs to be. Look around for accounts that pay higher interest and check for any charges.

Savings accounts are for frequent paying in but rare taking out. Save up for a specific purchase, then take out the amount you need to buy that particular thing. Money can also be taken out for emergencies (not invented excuses but real emergencies). Some accounts offer a bonus rate of interest if you leave your money in for a minimum time. Interest rates change over time and special offers expire, so check regularly to make sure you're still getting the best deal.

Make use of tax-free savings opportunities. Let your money benefit you, not the tax man.

Pension plans and long term savings accounts are for paying in only, until you retire and start living off them.

I used to keep spare change in a whisky bottle. It didn't earn any interest and then it was stolen. Now I put any money I have into a savings account where it can grow.

Can you afford not to save?

"I can't even make my money last until next pay day. You can't expect me to save!" Oh yes I can. Otherwise, how will you manage when disaster strikes?

The car fails its MOT. Without it you can't get to work. You have to spend a few hundred pounds to keep it on the road.

You develop an abscess in your tooth and run up large bills at the dentist.

Someone spills tomato soup down your only decent suit and it won't wash out.

Big or small, when the sudden unexpected need for money arrives, you need a way to cope.

Savings will take some of the fear out of life's twists and turns. It's scary on the edge of the cliff but if you know you have a safety rope, you'll feel secure and confident.

6 SHOPPING

Don't we all love a bit of retail therapy? It has become the god of the age. Shops are now open round the clock. Or of course, you can sit in the comfort of your armchair, day or night and order things from the four corners of the globe, all at the click of a button. It's just too easy and sooo tempting. Shopping is where most of your money goes and you'll get plenty of encouragement. Sounds obvious, but do you have a strategy for keeping a grip on it?

If you have problems keeping hold of your money and always come home from town with bags of new goodies, how can you get back in control? The threat is from advertising. Tackle it as one of the dangers of the wild that you have to survive. Your senses will be bombarded from every side. You need to move fast, dodge and weave and be armed with blinkers and ear defenders.

Get tough on the media

TV, websites, radio and magazines are full of adverts. There are billboards on the streets and leaflets arriving in your letterbox every day. Your email in-box is chock full of SPAM. TV programmes have product placement. You are even subjected to subliminal advertising without knowing it (check out YouTube[15]). You can't escape it but you can fight back.

The main aim of advertising is to make you unhappy! First they convince you that you have a problem. Then they tell you that their product will fix the problem. Like the sweet song of the Sirens luring sailors onto the rocks in Greek myths, advertising is designed to ruin you by selling false promises of happiness

---

15   www.youtube.com

which never come true. When you have saved or borrowed to buy their wares, you will find (after the initial buzz has worn off) that your life is still the same. Sellers just want your money and it is no concern of theirs whether or not you can afford to buy.

You might think that you just need the next item on the list to reach the level of happiness they portray. "If only I had a camcorder/dishwasher/Ferrari I'd be happy". Sorry - this doesn't work, as those with enough money to try it have discovered. You only get to be happy by being happy - not by having things. A sports car is a nice toy to play with but remember a contented child will enjoy a cardboard box while an unhappy child can be dissatisfied with the most expensive toys. We are all children inside. Let's rediscover the simple pleasures of life, most of which are free.

Defence Strategies

Avoid TV adverts
If you're watching TV and the adverts come on, hit mute (ear defenders), get up and look elsewhere (blinkers) and stretch or do something else (move fast) until they've finished. Actually, the happiest people I know either don't own a television or watch one only very rarely.

Beware free magazines
All magazines are subsidised by advertising. If you get one free, the advertisers have paid for the whole thing. The last one I checked had some sort of advertising on every page.

Focus on positives
It has been said that the secret of happiness is not having what you want; it's wanting what you already have. Put your efforts into being thankful for what you do have and enjoy your life. Try making a note of every single thing you can be thankful for. The sky is often stunning to look at if you take the time. As I wrote this, I enjoyed hearing a bird singing outside. Do it for a week or even a whole month. You'll be delighted how it changes the way you experience life when you concentrate only on what is good.

Shop less often

My favourite tip for spending less is, "Don't go shopping so often". It might sound too simple but the fewer trips you make to the shops, the less you'll spend. "But I'll just spend more the few times I do go!" I hear you cry. Perhaps, but not as much as many small trips added together. It is almost impossible to have a trip into town without buying something. How many days a week do you buy nothing? For me it's usually 4 or 5. If you only go to the shops once a week you'll have to stock up on important things like food and are less likely to buy unnecessary bits and pieces. It's a bit of 'out of sight, out of mind' (wear your blinkers). If you're always near shops, you will see things, then want them, then buy them.

Use a list

Keep a shopping list in the kitchen. As your supplies of a particular item run low, write it on the list. When you shop, buy all the items on the list. Then you should always have everything you need.

Of course, if you genuinely forget to list something that you need - buy it - but at least focussing on what you need will reduce the tendency to browse.

Look before you leap, buy later

An impulse buy often turns out to be a mistake. At the moment you first set eyes on a dazzling shirt or labour saving gadget, wild desire takes hold and you hand over your money on the spot. Later on, your star buy languishes in the wardrobe or gathers dust on a shelf. You wonder why you ever bought it and how you could stop yourself making the same mistake again. We all experience these emotional reactions to things that we see. Research shows that it's to do with the frontal lobe part of our brains and it isn't always easy to control our impulses.[16]

Unless it's on your list, don't buy anything as soon as you see it. Keep the money in your pocket and wait a while. Tell yourself you can have it, <u>if</u> you still want it at the end of the month <u>and</u> you have enough of that month's money left to buy it. (Don't tell yourself you can't have it, which would only introduce rebellion and increase the likelihood that you'll buy two!) Ask, "do I really <u>need</u> it?" and, "do I need it <u>now</u>?" Often you'll find your urge is not so strong another day. This 'cooling-off period' allows your brain time to digest all the pros and cons and make a better decision. You won't be aware of this going on, but it is.

---

16   BBC TV Horizon - how to make better decisions Feb 2008.

It's cheaper to decide you don't really like something before you buy it, than afterwards.

If you use mail order catalogues, mark the things that you might buy, but don't place the order. Marking the items gives you the satisfaction of having chosen them. It's a bit like window shopping. Put the catalogue away. When you get it out again, re-examine the things you marked. You'll see them in a whole new light and might no longer like or want them at all.

Use the same idea when surfing on-line; wait at least a week before going to the checkout page.

Limit the amount of time you have

The faster you move, the less likely you'll be trapped or snared. If you have the time to browse, they'll hook you and reel you in.

In town, use a car park with a time limit so that you only have a couple of hours to do all of your shopping. If you travel by bus or train, set yourself a departure time and stick to it. This concentrates the mind wonderfully and gives you the rest of the day to do other things.

Know what matters to you

There was a big fuss made some years ago about the amount of money that Elton John spent on flowers. But wait a minute, he can afford it and he likes flowers. The point is that you can buy whatever you choose with the money you have available. I'll let that bit sink in, *with the money you have available*. You will have identified in chapter 2 how much that is. What you use it for is entirely up to you. Knowing what matters to you really helps. It might not be flowers. Perhaps you want to eat organic food or if you drive a lot, having a comfortable car could be worth paying for.

When is a bargain not a bargain?

People love bargains, they always have. Going back thousands of years, the writer of Proverbs noticed:

"The customer always complains that the price is too high, but then he goes off and brags about the bargain he got."[17]

We love to think that we've got something for nothing.

Sales have proved so successful that the retail world has abandoned the once a year philosophy; someone is always having a sale. For us shoppers, sales are great aren't they?

17   Proverbs 20:14: The Good News Bible - Today's English Version, 1976, Collins/Fontana.

Why pay more than you have to? But you still need to think about what you're buying and why.

You see a pair of jeans in a shop window. The label says:

| was £34.99 |
| NOW £19.99 |
| **YOU SAVE £15!!!** |

Let's suppose you already have a pair of jeans and are in town to pay the electricity bill. You will not save £15 by buying the jeans. Instead you'll spend around £20 too much.

If, on the other hand you've gone into town because you need a pair of jeans, you have yourself a bargain!

If you wouldn't have bought something at full price it's unlikely to be a bargain for you even when it's reduced. Keep a sharp eye out too for the trick shops like to use of putting the price up for a while so that they can claim to have reduced it later.

A bargain could even be something that costs more if you compare high cost durable goods with cheap goods that wear out quickly. John Ruskin, the philosopher, said,

"It is unwise to pay too much but it is worse to pay too little. When you pay too much you lose a little money, that is all. When you pay too little you sometimes lose everything because the thing you bought was incapable of doing the thing it was bought to do. The common law of business balance prohibits paying a little and getting a lot; it cannot be done. If you deal with the lowest bidder it is well to add something for the risk you run. And if you do that, you will have enough to pay for the something better."[18]

18   This is usually attributed to John Ruskin 1819-1900 but the source has not been determined.

Second-Hand or Vintage?

Better even than sale goods are the bargains you can pick up in second-hand shops. A friend of mine found her most comfortable pair of shoes in one. They cost £5 instead of £120 and hadn't been worn. And remember that if you have good quality clothes that you don't want, you can sell them.

When I first bought a house, I did well for furniture and appliances through the local newspaper's "Classified Ads".

Food glorious food

We need to eat every day so shopping for food is a regular event. That makes it a good thing to take control of. Use your list. If you wander around looking at what's there, you'll buy all sorts of things that you might never eat. Pause for thought too before you snap up 'Buy One Get One Free' offers. A lot of food ends up being thrown away. Try lovefoodhatewaste.com for tips on getting the best from your food. I invented some of my favourite recipes by using up leftovers to make other meals.

I love buying fresh fruit and veg. at markets and local greengrocers. Check out farmers' markets and box schemes. You'll be supporting local producers who help resist the growing domination of the big supermarkets.

Check prices in different shops. 'Own brands' can be good value. Try them out. Some products you'll like as much as the market leader, saving you money. With other items, you might decide you're prepared to pay a bit extra for the one you enjoy much more.

Eat before you shop. If you're hungry, you'll impulse buy every tempting morsel you set eyes on.

Do you consider yourself to be rich enough to employ your own personal chef? That's what you're doing if you buy ready meals (to keep costs down they use cheap ingredients). Washed salad costs three times more than preparing your own; pre-mashed potatoes cost five times more. The most inflated price I found was ready sliced fruit for children which cost a whopping ten times more than whole fruit.

Ready meals are big business costing us over one billion pounds a year. Yes, life is busy these days. In Britain, we have the longest working hours in Europe so we don't want to spend half our evening slaving over a hot stove. But if you spend more than 20 minutes a day watching TV or on the computer, you have time to cook your own dinner. Cooking from scratch doesn't take much time or skill, is better for your health and cheaper. Here's the difference:

	Home made	Typical ready meal
Ingredients	Fresh vegetables Fresh meat or fish You pick the quality	Contents have been on the shelf for how long? They pick the quality Preservatives, colourings, salt, sugar, flavour enhancers
Time to prepare	20 minutes	10 minutes
Costs	Cost of fresh ingredients	Cost of ingredients plus chemicals and additives plus processing plus packaging plus marketing
How good for you?	Highly nutritious	Lacking in vitamins and enzymes due to ageing effects Your body has to work to process the toxins
Portion size	The amount you want	The amount they give you
Flavour	Tasty – the real thing	Lacking in taste and texture

Artificial drinks also cost a lot and often contain nasty chemicals and sugar. What your body really needs is water and that's free.

Being part Italian, I love bolognaise. It takes at least 3 hours to cook a good batch so every few months I put an evening aside and make two great pans full. Then I freeze it in portions to use as quick meals later on. I do the same with casseroles, fish pie, soup and home-made burgers.

As well as main meals, you can save a lot on lunches and snacks. Spending £5 a day on a sandwich and coffee might feel like a small amount, but by making your own for a year, you can save over £1,000.

If you're planning a special meal, prepare the menu in advance and put all the ingredients you need to buy on your list. Make sure that you stick to the list, rather than getting carried away buying special treats that are more extravagant than you intended.

There are exceptions that prove the rule. For special occasions, it's nice sometimes to buy the things you couldn't or wouldn't cook for yourself; those beautifully moulded smoked salmon nibbles stuffed with prawns, sumptuous desserts and iced cakes the shape of cartoon characters that the kids love. They can be marvellous when you're having a party. After all, you'd need a master class in piping to create all those extravagant creamy swirls.

Gadgets

We love gadgets these days. There are gadgets for every job you can think of plus a few you would never have imagined. But do we need them? And if we get them will we really use them?

Satnav is all the rage now but I know many people who have ended up in odd places or been instructed to take the most bizarre routes. Would it be simpler, cheaper and more rewarding to improve your map-reading skills?

Someone once bought me a food processor. I didn't want one and I knew that I was unlikely to take it out of its box every time I wanted to cut a few carrots or grate a bit of cheese (not to mention spending a quarter of an hour washing it up afterwards). I gave it to a friend who could make good use of it. I was also given a set of sharp knives in a wooden block; I use those every day. They do the jobs that dozens of gadgets claim to do. Simple tools are so versatile.

Clothes Shopping

Most of us have far more clothes than we need, some of which we hardly wear. If we're going to be honest with ourselves, we have all made mistakes - impulse buys which we immediately regretted. On the other hand, there will be a few favourite items in your wardrobe that you wear to destruction; the pair of trousers that don't feel tight when you sit down, the blue shirt that brings out the colour of your eyes, the old woolly jumper that's so warm and cosy. What is it about those few items that you love so much? If you can find out you can apply the same principles to all the garments you buy and you won't end up with lots of clothes but nothing to wear.

Fashion is an invention to make us spend more. New styles come in every season. Keeping up-to-date with the latest look is a sure way to spend a fortune. The more fashionable an item is today, the more unfashionable it will look tomorrow. You may get better value from something that costs more if you can use it for twice as long (I have a pair of leather boots over 10 years old) or it gives you a lot more pleasure.

Lifestyle matters. Everyone's different. Smart suits and polished shoes aren't going to be very useful if you live on a farm and love riding. On the other hand, if you have a high powered job, you need more than just a few pairs of faded denims and a scruffy T-shirt. It is nice to have something really special to wear if you're invited to a wedding or other occasion but the amount of money you spend should reflect the amount of time you'll actually wear it. So how do you spend your time?

Working

Relaxing at home

Seeing friends

Sport/hiking/gym/keep fit

Entertaining/eating out

Clubs/pubs

Gardening

Cleaning/DIY

Having looked at how you live - look at yourself. What type of person are you? What shape is your body? Not everyone looks good in leggings or straight skirts whatever the fashion mags may tell you is on-trend. Fashion gurus Trinny and Susannah warn of the frustration if you expect your shopping to change your life[19]. Your clothes will not turn you into the celebrity you saw wearing them.

---

19   What not to wear, Trinny Woodall and Susannah Constantine, Weidenfeld & Nicolson, 2003.

Think instead about the type of clothes you feel good wearing, maybe things you've worn when people have complimented you on your appearance. If you can afford it, have yourself colour analysed. If not learn what you can and work out for yourself what will make you look good. Once you know, your confidence will increase, you'll need to own fewer clothes to produce more outfits and your wardrobe will be coordinated. This is obviously a long term investment (it took me five years to convert my wardrobe) but it could be worth it.

- Sort out your wardrobe.
- Only get what you need.
- Avoid impulse buys and sales fever.
- Good quality clothes last longer (more expensive can be better value).
- For high fashion buy cheap.
- Get good shoes. Saves on pain and chiropody bills later.
- Buy clothes you can wash so you don't have to pay for dry-cleaning.

Internet Shopping

There's no limit to what you can buy on-line. Unfortunately, it removes you further from the feeling of spending. Cash can still help you reconnect with reality even though you can't use it to pay. Count out in cash the amount you intend to spend and hold it in your hand before you press the final button. Looking at real money will help you decide whether the thing you were going to buy is worth that much to you.

Shopaholic?

It's more like walking a tightrope than a cliff-top path for the shopaholic in town.

Shopping can become compulsive. It's an addiction similar to alcohol and drugs, with the same rush but none of the stigma or damage to your health. The effect on your finances however, can be devastating.

If you shop a lot, it's worth while finding out the reason. Examine what triggers a spending spree. If you spend money on things you don't need and feel bad afterwards, you may be trying to compensate for some other problem in your life.

Sometimes shopaholics have been found to suffer from low self-esteem or depression. Times of stress like divorce or job change can be the start of it. It's important to get help with any underlying emotional problems by working through them with a good counsellor or friend.

If you know your shopping runs away with you, your credit card company can help; ask them to lower your limit. There is a charity called the Consumer Credit Counselling

Service (CCCS)[20] that can give advice on money problems. Use cash (chapter 4) as a safety barrier to stop you going over the edge in moments of weakness. You don't have to come crashing onto the rocks every time you walk down the street.

---

20   Consumer Credit Counselling Service (CCCS).
www.cccs.co.uk

7 THE BIG ONES

In chapters 2 and 6, we thought about routine spending and how small amounts add up over time. Now we're going to consider houses and cars; the real big ones.

Your Home

Many of my survival tips involve only buying what you have enough money to pay for there and then. Houses are the exception; I don't know many people who have enough cash to buy a house. A mortgage is often a necessary loan. But the first question is, "Do I need to buy a house?" There is a strong culture of home ownership in Britain. In Europe it is much more common to rent. Buying a property may not be best for your situation.

Whether you're renting or buying, when you're deciding what price of home to look for, think about the long list of outgoings in Table 1, chapter 2. Your home is one of your biggest costs but you need enough left for all those other things too. Set the amount based on what you can afford.

Renting

There are lots of things to think about if you decide to rent and lots of questions to be answered. Will you need a furnished or unfurnished property? Will you share with other people to spread the costs? What are the terms of the tenancy? Who is the landlord and can you find out about his situation? One landlord I rented from decided to sell and I had to get out at very short notice. You want to find a place that's right for you with a lease that allows you to stay as long as you need.

Lodging

Even more cost effective than renting, would you consider being someone's lodger? It's really renting only a room rather than a whole place for yourself. I lodged for a year when working in the south of England, had a room in a much nicer house than I would have been able to afford otherwise and also made new friends.

Buying

If you decide you do want to buy, think about the timing. Would it be best to do it now or later? You could find that renting for a while and saving a larger deposit allows you to enter the housing market in a better state. Should you buy alone or is there someone who could buy part of the house with you? Could you take in a lodger to offset some of your costs?

With a mortgage, remember that interest rates go up and down unpredictably. If you buy at a time when interest rates are low, be prepared for increases. Keep your borrowing small enough that you can cope when they go up again. This way you won't face, possibly the most devastating crisis of all, the loss of your home[21]. It's frightening to know that over 40,000 homes were repossessed in 2008[22]. To make sure, you could take out a fixed interest rate mortgage for a few years. That way you'll know exactly how much you'll pay each month and you'll know you can afford it.

Everyone wants to sell you a mortgage these days, not just building societies and banks but even supermarkets. Take advantage and shop around a bit. The choice is somewhat mind boggling but stick at it until you can't stand any more and then choose the best deal.

Lenders will be eager to help you - but beware! They'll be happy to give you huge mortgages, although thankfully less than a

---

21   Contact a charity such as Shelter (www.shelter.org.uk) if you have housing problems.

22   Council of Mortgage Lenders. www.cml.org.uk

few years ago. The more you borrow, the more money they'll make out of you. Don't fall for 'cash back' offers you don't need. These are just a way of getting you to take a bigger loan. Stick to your limit and don't be bullied into taking more. They don't care if high repayments will make your life difficult. If you default they will kick you out and sell your house. They can't lose. It's up to you to protect your own best interests.

Think hard and take lots of advice before committing yourself to the biggest financial outlay you will ever make.

Living in it

As well as the costs of the place itself, you can save money on all the associated services you'll need. If you didn't shop around for energy providers, insurance, telephone service etc. as part of the work you did in chapter 2, do it now.   Putting some effort into getting good deals on these ongoing costs can add up because you'll be saving month after month.

For example, if you spend a lot on calls and texts from your mobile 'phone, think a bit about what those calls are, who they are to and when you make them. Could you keep in touch just as well by calling from a land line in the evening or would a contract with a number of included calls and texts be better value for you? Extras like ring tones can add up to a lot over a year.

Making a house your home

Once you have somewhere to live, the scope for spending money on improving it is endless.   There are loads of magazines dedicated to furniture, furnishings, decorating and gardening, plus endless style and "makeover" programmes on TV. People want new looks and they want them fast. It's easy to get carried away and spend £100s or even £1,000s on décor.

As a lodger you'll be limited in what you can do, if anything. Tenancy agreements will stipulate what lengths you can go to if you rent. As a home owner, it's up to you to limit yourself. I don't expect you to sit on a packing box like I did, but you could try freecycle.org.uk or the Furniture Re-use Network (frn.org.uk). Paint is cheaper than wallpaper. Ready-made curtains cost less than made-to-measure and can sometimes be cheaper than making your own.

Gardens can soak up even more money than home improvements. With a bit of patience, you can cheaply grow the plants you want from seed. Buying full grown ones from garden centres is like employing your own gardener. Talk to your neighbours over the fence and you might be able to give each other plants. Ponds are tranquil and attract wildlife but you don't have to splash out on coy carp. We had a fish thief in our area a while ago who stole several coy, worth up to £2,000 each. Little goldfish are cheap and fun to watch.

Think about what you really need and take into account how long you intend to live where you are. The average is only a few years. Then you'll have to start all over again somewhere else. Spend enough to make your house your home but keep enough for priority payments (see chapter 3).

Cars and motorbikes

Like houses, it may not be the best solution for you to own a car. They're a positive liability in London where there's nowhere to park, appalling traffic and lots of good public transport. They're an absolute necessity in the country where the nearest bus stop might be 3 miles away with a service only twice a day.

Where you live in relation to the places you need to go is obviously the most important factor in deciding what you'll need in the way of transport. How often do you travel and where to? Then think about who will travel with you and what you'll have to carry. When working out what sort of car/bike to buy, start at the bottom by asking, "What do I need?" You'll probably end up with a much cheaper one than if you started at the top saying, "What is the most I can afford?". It will still get you from A to B.

Could you use taxis? It may sound like insane extravagance for a skint person, but you can get an awful lot of taxi rides for the cost of running a car. (Remember all the car related costs in chapter 2. As well as buying it in the first place there are tax, insurance, servicing, repairs and fuel.)

What about joining a car club (e.g. see carplus.org.uk) that enables you to have a car to use when you need it for less cost than standard hire? If you don't use a car very often, it could make sense; you would need to compare costs.

Could you car-share? Groups of people going to work together every day is very cost-effective. Your workplace may put people in contact or you might try one of the very many car sharing websites.

Buying Cars

At the risk of incurring the wrath of all car manufacturers everywhere, I recommend that you don't buy new cars. The initial depreciation simply is not compensated for by the kudos of having the latest registration number. Second hand cars are much better value for money and someone else will have sorted out any early teething problems. Ask someone who knows about cars to come and look at it with you. If you don't know anyone, you can have an inspection done by the AA or RAC to check that the car is sound.

Change as infrequently as you can. A boss of mine bought only 3 cars in 30 years and saved £10,000s. He kept them until they'd done up to 150,000 miles before thinking about getting another.

If you do decide to buy a car, get one that you can afford to pay for in cash. This might mean picking up an old banger for a few hundred pounds, knowing that it won't last very long.

Finance on an expensive car will be a millstone round your neck and can cost you a packet. It's a loan under another name, see the example in chapter 8 where a £14,015 car on finance costs £16,265 in total.

Now if they offered you £2,250 off you'd be more than pleased. But £2,250 too much???? It doesn't look attractive to me. Having worked for my pay, I don't want to give it away paying over the odds; do you? Also, you'll still be paying out those £200 monthly amounts over four years later. Way before then you'll need money for other things.

The type of car you buy affects more than just the initial outlay. There are different tax brackets depending on CO_2 emissions; insurance costs vary enormously as do servicing and repairs. Shop around and you could save quite a bit.

Save on fuel by driving more smoothly to improve your MPG. Advice on economical motoring is an addition to the driving test for 2009. Manage the space around you and avoid sharp breaking or acceleration as a heavy right foot can easily cost you 10-20% extra.

Regular servicing costs money but keeps the car in good condition for longer. Looking after your car means that it's safer for you to drive, and should need fewer repairs saving more money.

You can even save money on the little things. I've always enjoyed washing my car with a bucket of hot soapy water and a sponge; it costs next to nothing compared to a car-wash. It's kinder to your paintwork too which might help you get a better price when you sell.

8 CREDIT AND DEBT

Here's another danger to survive. This time it's sharks, so you need your wits about you.

If you have money problems does it make loans and credit cards hard to get? Not at all! You'll be constantly bombarded by offers through junk mail, email, TV adverts, shops and banks.

A book like this simply had to have a whole chapter dedicated to credit because of the misery millions of people suffer due to their debts. Adverts for credit make me see red - with anger. Someone is getting very rich out of you and me, devouring us like sharks as we cling to the rocks of financial ruin. It's a scandal - daylight robbery made legal - are you equipped to defend yourself against the onslaught?

Like the adverts that lure you into buying more, you can be enticed into taking loans by images of smiling people buying things they can't afford. It's a deadly trap.

Get a hold of your finances and don't allow your bank or credit providers to take control of you. The banks provide a service to you but want to make as much out of you as they can.

So who's looking after your best interests? Your money belongs to you; so do your debts. It's down to you.

Buying using credit and loans

Credit sounds like such a good idea. Have it now, pay for it later.

If you can get interest free credit and you're good at managing your finances, then consider it. But first think about this. If you were still paying now for something you got four years ago, how would you feel? It's a burden that drags you down. It could be less painful to pay up front.

For credit with interest, decide whether it is worth the extra cost to have the thing sooner. The rate (APR) may be listed as 17% but what does that mean? Over the repayment period how much extra will it add up to? Ask them to work it out for you in the shop - you could be in for a nasty surprise.

In the last chapter we looked at buying cars; I got the following example from a car showroom.

You see a car with a price tag of £14,000

If you buy outright, that's what you pay - or perhaps a bit less for a cash sale.

Finance offered was a deposit of £5,600 followed by £200 a month at 16.3%

Does £200 a month sound like a good deal? Affordable? Easy?

It will take longer than 4 years to make the car yours.

The total amount paid is £16,265.

That's nearly £2,300 more than the price!

OK - so now you know how much it really costs. Are you willing to pay £16,300 for a £14,000 car?

If the car had a sign on saying £2,300 off, you'd be pleased. But £2,300 extra???? Would you jump at the chance to pay so much more?

With the same deposit to start with, if you put aside £200 a month in a savings account, you will have the £14,000 you need in just over 3 years, saving you one year. The interest paid to you on your savings will add to the payments you make, so you will save not £2,300 but nearer £3,000 compared with the loan. And you'll probably get a discount for a cash sale saving you even more.

Sellers and lenders get away with it simply because few people work out the total cost. They won't always explain to you the way that your debt can grow. The advertising blurb will concentrate on the size of your weekly payment. "You pay only £50 a week." They act as if they're doing you a favour. You can have anything you want and it will hardly cost you a thing. In truth, the smaller your repayments, the greater your total spend and the longer you'll be paying.

For a £5,000 bank loan at 7.4%		
Monthly payment	Time to pay off loan	Total cost
£433	1 year	£5,200
£155	3 years	£5,600
£100	5 years	£6,000

Always calculate the real cost of a loan before you decide to go ahead. Check the small print. If they try to baffle you with jargon, take someone along who understands, to help and advise you.

Some loans are secured against your house. If for any reason you can't keep up the payments, you will lose your home. Remember, there are no certainties in life (except death and taxes[23]). Even if you can manage the payments at the beginning, your

---

23   Benjamin Franklin, 1706-1790.

circumstances could change in the future, leaving you in trouble.

Be careful who you borrow from. There are illegal money lenders to beware of. Regional teams are fighting against them on your behalf; contact your local authority for more information. Local Credit Unions are cheaper and safer than loan sharks.

Today's culture is not one of waiting. People are impatient. But if you've managed without something up to now, is it really going to have a major effect on your life to wait a bit longer while you save up? The answer is up to you. As always, go in with your eyes open.

Credit and Store Cards

Plastic is so useful isn't it? So convenient; so easy; SO DANGEROUS.

When I was a child I used to think that cheques were money. If Mum ran out of money she could simply write a cheque to pay for something. I expect that children today start with the same misconception about plastic. Eventually it dawned on me that cards are simply ways of spending the money you already have in the bank. Except, of course, that you can buy things with credit cards even if you haven't got the money in the bank. It's only later that the company comes calling for what's due.

Credit cards don't cost you anything if you pay off the full balance each month. If you use them well and purchase only what you can pay for, they're a convenient way to buy things.

On the down side, it doesn't really feel like spending when you use plastic. Parting with fistfuls of notes is much more difficult. You can't pay with cash on the Internet of course. Use the tip from chapter 6 to increase the impact by holding the amount of cash in your hand that you are intending to spend on-line. This will connect you to the spending experience and might make you think again.

In Britain the credit card debt is over £50 billion with the total unsecured debt around £230 billion![24] Let me express this another way; that is £230,000,000,000!!!!!!!! Don't let any of it be yours.

If you have outstanding amounts on your credit cards at the moment, look hard at the interest when your statement arrives. You don't ever get something for nothing but you do get nothing for something when you pay interest on debts. If you weren't paying this

---

24   Credit Action. www.creditaction.org.uk

interest, what could you buy that you really want?

If you have several cards with debts on all of them, choose one card with a good rate and transfer all your debts to it. Some banks offer special deals on transferred balances (at least in the short term). It's another ploy they use to get your custom but you can use it to your advantage. Then get rid of all the other cards. Cancel them and cut them up!

If you have savings that are earning a low rate of interest and debts with a high rate of interest, use some of your savings to pay off the debts (keeping some back as your emergency lifeline). This applies to any debts e.g. car loans, credit cards, student loans, mortgage, bank loans.

Some types of debt are justifiable and necessary like money borrowed to start a business, buy a house or get you through college. It's consumer debt that's the killer. The things you buy last for less time than the debt so you can never catch up. The interest rates are high and you have little to show for your pains at the end. Use good old cash (see chapter 4) to help you get back in control.

Debt Repayment

The enormity of the problem might overwhelm you, so break it down into pieces that you can manage. When John Bird had to dig a large piece of ground as a child, he first marked it out into squares small enough to tackle[25].

If you're badly in debt, you're in a serious situation. People who fall off cliffs always need rescue experts to help them.

---

25   How to Change Your Life in 7 Steps, John Bird (founder of the Big Issue magazine), Vermillion, 2007.

It can feel daunting admitting that you have a problem but it's the responsible thing to do. Going to speak to someone is probably the hardest step and things usually get easier once you've done it. The Citizens' Advice Bureau is a good place to start and they'll tell you about organisations that give advice specifically on debt (see Resources).

Help yourself as much as you can. Consider taking on extra work. Sell things that you don't need (using car-boot sales, eBay, newspaper ads etc.).

Pay off the debt with the highest interest rate first. The more money you can pay back to your creditors, the faster the pain will go. Delay just increases the size of your debt through accumulated interest, even if you don't spend a single penny more. (Interest is being added all the time on your outstanding balance, so if you can double your payments, you'll clear the debt much faster than in half the time.)

Get mobilised and climb off the rocks back up the cliff to the path. You'll start feeling better long before you get to the top and when you clear the last pound you'll experience a great sense of freedom and self esteem.

9 CHILDREN

If you weren't skint before, you could soon be heading that way when you hear the patter of tiny feet. It's an unavoidable fact of life that children are EXPENSIVE!

You're the leader of the survival expedition now. Your kids rely on you to provide for them and keep them safe. Once you have dependants, life insurance is important and a will is essential, see chapter 14.

Not only is there a multitude of extra expenses, but someone will have to be there to look after 'baby'. Unless you're lucky enough to have wonderful family members nearby who'll enjoy looking after your kids, that means paying for child care (there are voucher schemes that you may be able to use). Or you have to stop working and therefore earning.

You may fully intend to resume working after maternity or paternity leave. But once you've been at home for a while with the amazing little human being you've created, you might change your mind. Do you know whether you could cope financially if you gave up your job? It's well worth doing the thinking and planning for a range of options in advance. Afterwards you might not have the time or energy to work things through rationally.

Babies

Babies require a huge amount of paraphernalia so this is not a time to be snobby. Accept prams, cots, car seats, toys and clothes from family and friends.

Always hungry, babies love breast milk; it's free and provides protection against disease. Nutritionally, it's the perfect food and infinitely superior to any bought formula milk.

Babies start small but they grow with amazing speed. It's tempting to buy loads of adorable tiny clothes but many of them will only be worn once before you need something bigger. Look out for local 'clothes-swap' events for baby and toddler sizes. Charity shops often have good second hand baby clothes, some of which will be 'as new'.

Toddlers like playing with wooden spoons, boxes, tins, pebbles, shells and all sorts of ordinary objects. They don't need expensive, sophisticated toys. Don't force children to grow up too quickly; let them play.

Kids

Older children need entertaining. Make the most of what's available free. Just think how many games you can play with a piece of paper and a pencil. Build up a craft kit with wrapping paper, boxes, tubes, buttons, ribbon and lots of glue and sticky tape. Have a dressing-up box of old clothes for games and made up theatre. Kids love getting in a sticky mess baking, so you can have fun while teaching them how to cook.

A library is a wondrous place for a child. So many books, just for them, that they can choose and take home by the armful to read, then bring them back and get some more. I still remember the thrill of it. Libraries also do reasonably priced DVD hire.

Some museums and art galleries have free admission. These are great places for learning that you can enjoy and appreciate things without having to own them.

An afternoon gardening or playing in a park is great fun and good exercise. Boys can amuse themselves for hours with games of skill, skimming stones or kicking a football around.

Teenage girls enjoy having their own clothes-swap parties (now back on trend) where a group of friends all get new outfits for no money.

Toys

Children have great imagination and can play with anything so don't think that you have to spend a fortune to keep them happy. With young ones, the toy itself may be missed completely in the euphoria of rustling coloured paper and a cardboard box. Boxes, as I remember well, can become a boat, car, train, house….

The first present opened at Christmas is a wondrous thing and could be enjoyed all day if someone didn't actually prod the pile of other gifts into view. It's easy to assume that if one toy is fun to play with, two or three or four will be better, but young children can end up sitting confused and tearful in a heap, so overwhelmed they can't enjoy anything.

The simplest toys give the most lasting pleasure because they change with the child's imagination. A TV or film-based, one-off toy showing a character or vehicle, is always just that. It's too specific to become anything else and that will be its limitation. This is why blocks and modelling clay have so much appeal; they are what you create with them each day and you can buy extra to add to what you have.   Games and jigsaws cost almost nothing in charity shops and car boot sales.

Generally a child won't have a favourite toy. They get their fun from the game they're giving their attention to at any particular moment.   Their favourite thing will be whatever they're playing with NOW.

Shopping and Pester Power

Everywhere is a temptation danger-zone. Even supermarkets sell DVDs, mobile 'phones and toys.   Explain what child-targeted advertising is about and why they don't need to fall for it.   It's about companies selling more things in order to boost profits for their shareholders.   It is not driven by your child's best interests. You may be surprised by how well even young children can understand this.

Peer pressure will be a problem, as it is for ourselves, but it's harder for a child to resist. Kids use the enormously effective pester-power, nagging constantly if designer trainers, CDs and electronic games are not provided. Keeping up with the latest trends and styles is the easiest way in the world to waste money. Designs constantly change so that there is never an end to the spending, no matter what you buy today.

If you feel compelled to rush out and buy what your neighbour has, don't be surprised when your offspring want to keep up with the Joneses of the playground. Resist the culture that says you only matter for what you do or what you have. Personal qualities such as honesty, humour and consideration for others are much more important than fleeting 'street cred'. Value your kids for who they are and help them develop their self-esteem.

Many food products are aimed specifically at children. Unfortunately, most of them are unhealthy in the extreme: sugary breakfast cereals, drinks and desserts full of colourings and preservatives, endless sweets and crisps (use shops that have a choice of checkouts without sweets). Some of the behavioural problems that are now becoming so common have been linked to these foods.

What kids eat becomes the building material for growing bodies. For health and strength they need natural, high quality nutrients, not sugar and toxic chemicals. Fill them up on proper meals and give them fresh or dried fruit instead of letting them snack on things that appeal because of their packaging. Since you will always have unsuitable produce under their noses wherever you go, it is important to teach your kids to discriminate and be responsible.

Attitude and education

Handling money is an essential life skill. Why don't they teach this stuff in school? Millions of people are out there struggling and learning the hard way. I guess if you're reading this, you might be one of them too. Your kids don't have to be. Remember you're the expedition leader, so teach your children the basic skills of money management and you'll give them a firm foundation for survival.

Your children will pick up your attitudes. The way you talk about things, even casually, can be major learning for them. If your kids see that the way you handle money helps you to enjoy life with fewer worries they'll learn from that. Let them see you be independent and enjoy your own style.

Some parents put all their time and energy into work. They chase extra money at the expense of time spent with their family. The lesson the children receive is that they are less important than money and this can damage their self esteem.

Albert Schweitzer[26] said "There are only three ways to teach a child: The first is by example, the second is by example, the third is by example." Never underestimate the power of your influence.

Kids quickly learn to enjoy getting and spending money, whether it's pocket money given to them or pay for work. Poor children know how awful it is to have too little and can't imagine there being a down side to having too much. But as Richard Foster observed, for children the power to buy can

26   Albert Schweitzer, theologian and philosopher, 1875-1965.

be heady stuff[27]. Sadly, rich kids sometimes use money to humiliate those around them; just as they see adults doing the same.

Chapters 3 and 10 look at the contrast between different parts of the world. Children as well as adults need to be reminded about their wealth relative to the world's poor. Chapter 3 considers happiness and how it isn't related to what we buy and own. Don't spoil your kids; teach them that money is useful and necessary but it isn't the most important thing.

Limits

Children respond well to consistently applied boundaries and rules. Start saying "NO" early on so they learn that you can't always have what you want in life. Explain the difference between needing and wanting. For older kids,

---

27   Money, Sex and Power, Richard J Foster, Hodder & Stoughton, 1985.

explain that money isn't limitless. Teach them moderation, restraint and how to make choices. Perhaps they can have one comic, which do they like best? For younger children, set simple rules and stick to them.

Be careful what expectations you build. If you get kids a treat on three consecutive trips to the shops, that's enough to be thrown back at you as, "but you **always** get me a treat when we go shopping".

Giving kids what they want because you can't stand them whining, is a good way to reward and hence encourage more whining! Indulging bad behaviour and allowing yourself to be bullied into buying things you can't afford will ruin you and them.

Be honest. If you'd love to get something your child wants but you can't afford it, say so. Don't pretend you think they shouldn't have it if they've asked for something sensible. Compliment them for their good judgement, explain that it's too expensive and make sure they know you still love them.

The Piggy Bank

Start kids saving young. It's a skill that they'll benefit from all through their lives. When you're little, it's easy and fun to put pennies through a slot into a piggy bank.

I remember my first piggy bank and it wasn't a pig. It was shaped like a book bound in pale blue leather with shiny gold metal sides where the page edges would be. Interlocking prongs across the slot stopped you getting the coins out yourself and it was locked with a key held by the bank. When I went there to get my money, I was sad to find out that the bank owned the box and I couldn't have it any more. I never liked the plastic horse-shaped box they gave me instead even though they said I could keep it and open it myself whenever I wanted.

Later on I had my own building society account. By then I was working a few hours a week as a shop assistant. I learned that banks and building societies pay interest on savings so, as well as what I saved, they gave me extra money too.

What mattered most was that I learned about saving and have always done it. Every few months my friend and I would go into town on the train with the money we'd saved. It felt grown up to pay for our own lunch in a restaurant and buy music, clothes and presents for friends and family with our own money.

You could open a savings account for each child when they are born. The Government will provide money to start a Child Trust Fund[28] (money not accessible until they are 18). Relatives could give money instead of baby clothes and Christening presents.

Avoid the credit mentality that causes adults so many difficulties and teach your kids to save first and buy later. There's a delicious anticipation in waiting for something while you save up for it and great satisfaction when you get it. The other bonus is that by the time you have saved up, you know whether you really want something and will avoid wasting money on impulse buys.

Giving

They may be young and everything they have comes from you, but don't assume that

---

28   www.childtrustfund.gov.uk

children are not capable of giving. At my first school we were each given a collection box, the shape of a house, made of papier mache. They could only be opened when the teacher cut the bottom off at the end of the year. We gave to Barnardos and even had a school trip to an orphanage to see how our money was helping improve the lives of needy children. Stirring stuff at six years old, it taught me that someone is always worse off and that I could do something important, however small.

Each year there's the Operation Christmas Child 'shoebox appeal' which many schools take part in.

One little boy didn't know how to open his Christmas Child shoebox and he picked a hole in the end with his finger. Just there was a pencil, which came out through the hole. He sat holding it in wonder, just looking. He had never had anything so wonderful. When a helper came and took the lid off the box and showed him the sweets and toys, he was overwhelmed and could not believe that it was all for him.

A shoebox is not large but a few stationery items, toiletries, sweets and toys can bring a big smile to the face of a child who has never received a present before in its life.

Other ways of giving include taking old toys and books to hospitals or giving them to charity shops. Blue Peter appeals over the decades have shown how collecting simple things like bottle tops can capture the imagination and philanthropic spirit.

First work experience

A child's first experience of work is often the pleasure of helping with tasks in the home. I used to love cleaning out my grandmother's kitchen cupboards and washing her collection of miniature bottles. At home I enjoyed sweeping the garage. I did these things because I liked to help and it was fun. I knew a lady who didn't give her three children pocket money but paid them for household chores - cleaning, preparing meals etc. Decide on the best approach for you and your children.

From the age of 12, I had a variety of paid jobs; a paper round, factory work and a shop assistant. Earning money for doing work can boost children's confidence and give them a taste of financial independence. It also helps them appreciate the work that their parents have to do to bring in money. The job itself will allow them to mix with people from different backgrounds and will build skills like customer service, discipline, punctuality and politeness. And they'll discover how enjoyable and fulfilling work can be.

Holidays

Taking a whole family away on holiday can be an expensive business. The main pleasure is being together, away from home, work and school. Where you go and what you do are less important. Camping and caravanning or staying with friends can be great fun. Do inexpensive activities like walking.

Prices are highest during school holidays so book last minute deals when tour operators are trying to fill quotas. You could do a house swap with another family so you only have the cost of travelling. There are lots of holiday exchange websites and Which?[29] has a useful guide about this type of holiday.

Students and young adults

The biggest expense parents might have is if they pay for their children to go on to higher education. More and more people are going to university now and after fees and living costs they can expect to leave with debts of

---

29   www.which.co.uk

£10,000s. This is a terrible way to start your adult life although the higher salary they might earn with a degree should help to pay it off. One alternative is to start work first and have the employer pay the fees to get qualifications, or to do an apprenticeship.

Sometimes young adults leave home but haven't really grown up. They keep going back to their parents expecting to be bailed out when they get into trouble. Teaching them about money from a young age will help them more than giving handouts later. You'll have helped them learn to cope so that they too can be survivors.

10 GO GREEN

The green bandwagon

Being environmentally friendly is very fashionable at the moment, which I think is great. The downside is the amount of misleading information around. It's called 'green-wash' and in the same way as most advertising, is designed to dupe you into spending your money.

Why should it cost you a fortune to be green? It shouldn't. A lot of the marketing blurb is seriously misleading, so take everything with a pinch of salt and don't believe what you're told. The only way round this one is to stay alert to it and to learn what you can so that you can see through false claims.

Here are the basic principles for green living.

Reduce

The main green thing to do of course is buy less stuff. I find it ironic that as green issues have gained prominence, manufacturers have jumped on the bandwagon and now use the environment in their attempts to sell you more and more.

If something like your kettle stops working, you will need to replace it. But how important is it to change a perfectly functional blue one for a white one, just to suit your colour scheme?

Many items can be repaired. Buttons can be sewn back on. Moth holes in a good sweater can be invisibly darned. Broken toys can be glued back together.

Worth bearing in mind in a book about not having enough money is the fact that we're richer than almost all the rest of the population of this planet. People in the developing world use a fraction of what we use in the wealthy and consumerist west, with 20% of the world's population using 80% of its resources[30]. When Fiona Castle (wife of the late Roy Castle) went to Peru, she found the people were happy but they had very few possessions[31]. If you compare what you have with people from many countries in the world, you already own more than they could imagine.

There are a number of costs associated with everything you buy: the labour and energy used in making it; the raw materials it's made from; transport (which also causes pollution); storage (particularly if refrigerated); and disposal, which costs more all the time.

---

30   Cumbria Business Environment Network.
31   Living Simply, Fiona Castle and Jan Greenough, Kingsway Communications Ltd, 2006.

As well as the things themselves, this is also true of the packages they come in. Until recently, manufacturers were package mad but thankfully some are cutting back on extravagant containers. A classic example of overdoing presentation is the Easter egg. If you compare the cost per ounce/gram of Easter egg chocolate to an ordinary bar, you'll discover that all that fancy packaging costs you a fortune. Of course I'm not against buying the odd Easter egg once a year but they are a splendid example of a principle which covers the whole range of consumer goods. Keep your eyes open when you shop.

It makes sense to support local firms and buy regional produce, particularly food. Growing your own is even better. It means you can walk out of the door and pick the best and freshest fruit and veg. you've ever tasted.

Buying less is of course very cost effective as well as environmentally friendly. Cutting down on what you buy protects your pocket and your planet.

Having reduced how much you buy, think too about what happens next to things you no longer need. Here are the options ranked in order of effectiveness.

Reuse

Reuse is the best way to make an item give value for money. Reuse even the little things like envelopes and supermarket carrier bags. Bath and dishwater can be used to water the garden (very useful in the south where the hosepipe bans are rarely lifted). If you're on a water meter you'll save money as well as reducing your environmental impact.

You don't have to reuse an item yourself. Take something you no longer want to a charity shop, sell it at a car-boot sale or on eBay or give it away on www.freecycle.co.uk or www.frn.org.uk (furniture recycle network) and someone else can get extra life out of it. I was short of money when I got my first house and it was furnished almost entirely from things advertised in the local paper.

Recycle

Recycling of household waste is something our grandparents took for granted and is now enjoying a revival. It isn't as good as reuse because there are always energy costs involved. So, for example the reuse of milk bottles is about as environmentally sound as you can get whereas taking bottles to the local bottle bank is a good second best. Most areas now have recycling centres or collection schemes for glass, paper, cans, clothing and plastic.[32]

Glass is a great material to recycle because the final product is as good as the original. The same is true of metal. Recycling of paper is not always so successful in terms of quality and because of the energy and chemicals involved. Fleece is so soft and fluffy, it's amazing to think it's made from old plastic bottles!

Refuse

Refuse is the last resort. There is a landfill crisis in Britain. We produce so much waste that we're running out of places to put it. So before throwing anything away, pause for a moment and ask yourself whether there's an alternative.

---

32   www.recyclenow.com

An old fashioned phrase that needs to come back on trend is, 'waste not, want not.' Buy what you need and use it all. Why take money out of your pocket and walk down the street putting it in every waste bin you pass?

When my council invested in wheelie bins, people complained that they were too small. Where does all this rubbish come from that needs to be taken away? We buy it at the shops each week.

11 INVESTMENTS

By investments, I mean things that will pay for themselves after an initial outlay. If you're keen to invest money with banks, building societies or on the stock market, you're past the skint stage and need a financial adviser - and that's not me.

Here are a few ideas, just to start you thinking. With gas and electricity prices rising at an alarming rate, I've included several energy saving measures. Before doing any of these things think about whether you can afford the up-front cost and work out how long the pay-back time is.

Energy

Double Glazing	You don't have to fit the best for it to work well. Even secondary panels held on with magnetic strips make a big difference. Saves money on heating bills, reduces damp and insulates sound.
Loft and cavity wall insulation	Insulation almost always pays for itself in a short time and there are grants to help pay for it.
Low energy bulbs	Energy saving light bulbs use much less electricity than conventional light bulbs.
Shower	Showers use a fraction of the water that you would have put in a bath.
Wood burning stove	At 80 % efficient, these are one of the best ways of warming your home. They're carbon neutral, toasty warm and the flames are relaxing to watch.
Extra driving lessons Advanced motorist	Learning how to drive better can save you petrol by improving your fuel consumption.[33] You'll also be safer on the road.

33   www.cleangreencars.co.uk

Food

Gardens, allotments, window boxes and pots	Growing things to eat is satisfying and the produce is good for you. Seeds are cheap and you can often swap plants with other gardeners. Herbs will grow in pots on the window-sill if you have no garden.

Work related

Training, coaching and personal development	Training can help you get a better paid job. Almost any activity that helps you grow and develop as a person is worthwhile.
Books	There are countless books on any subject you might need to help your work and the library can often order less common ones. For example, to be organised and get more done try: Taming the Paper Tiger, Barbara Hemphill. Eat that Frog, Brain Tracey Touch Typing in 10 Hours, Ann Dobson.

Personal

Books	Hundreds of books are available on increasing your personal effectiveness. For example try: The 7 Habits of Highly Effective People, Stephen R. Covey.
Metabolic Type Testing	Find out what foods are right for your individual body chemistry.[34] Eating right for your type will bring enormous health benefits.
Sewing skills	Gaining some sewing skills may not make you a tailor/dressmaker but will allow you to repair, alter and embellish your clothes.
Happiness courses	There are lot of courses on happiness. Try Robert Holding who also wrote the book Happiness Now.[35]
Colour analysis	Improve your wardrobe, and reduce costly mistakes.[36]
Alexander Technique lessons	Learn to use your body. Move with grace and avoid pain and medical costs later in life.[37]

34   www.personal-nutrition.co.uk
35   www.happiness.co.uk
36   www.ColourMeBeautiful.co.uk
37   www.stat.co.uk

Recreation

Dumb-bells Exercise DVDs	Instead of paying to go to a gym, buy a few weights and exercise at home. To vary your routine, rent DVDs from the library or buy them from charity shops.
Life Membership of the National Trust or English Heritage	Visit beautiful houses and gardens free (with a guest) for the rest of your life.

The one I've made most use of and would never be without is car recovery. When I was skint I bought cars that cost a few hundred pounds and they broke down - often! I probably owe my breakdown company a lifetime's membership and I'm sure they breathed a sigh of relief when I got my first decent vehicle.

You get the idea. Use your imagination to find ways to make your money work for you.

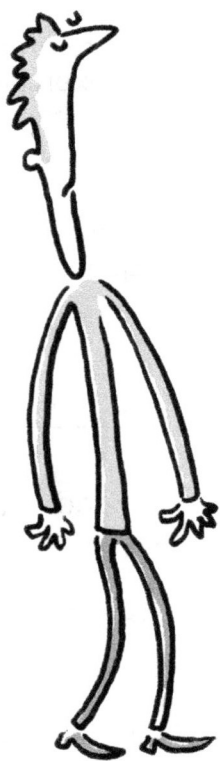

12 SLIMMING

What on earth has slimming to do with money? Ah well, quite a lot, otherwise it wouldn't be such an enormous industry. Just take a good look at the advertising you see over the next few days.

Our modern lifestyle has left the majority of us carrying more weight than is good for us. A bit extra and we're cuddly but more than that and let's be honest, it doesn't feel good and taken to extremes, it poses a serious risk to our health. Consequently millions of people go on diets every year in the hope of regaining their figure.

Preying on our health fears and image insecurities, a multi million pound industry gladly takes our money in exchange for creams, pills and potions (sometimes called shakes these days but often still just a drink made of dubious chemicals).

We want to slim without sacrifice, to change the shape of our bodies without changing our eating habits, to wave a magic wand instead of having to think and take responsibility for our own health. Each year we spend £2 billion in the UK on weight loss products[38] plus the NHS spends approaching £50 million[39] on prescribed slimming pills. It's interesting that the US, the most obese population in the world, with two out of three people overweight[40], also spends the most on weight loss products and services (estimated at $50-90 billion)[41].

38   www.bbc.co.uk
39   www.dailymail.co.uk/health/article-473467/NHS-spending-1m-week-slimming-pills-obese-Britons.html
40   www.who.int/infobase/reportviewer.aspx?rptcode=ALL&surveycode=102586a1&dm=5
41   www.mercola.com

There are multitudes of companies out there offering us gimmicks and diets that claim to shed the pounds without deprivation. If these products worked, you would get slimmer and stop buying them. Unfortunately, as many disappointed customers can testify, it's a myth.

Weight loss success

I've been overweight twice and I wasn't happy at all. My clothes didn't fit and I felt lethargic. Eventually I decided I had to do something. I joined a Scottish Slimmers[42] class (in England) which provided lots of support. I kept a record of everything I ate to raise my awareness and help me understand what was happening. It's the same principle we used in chapter 2 with our money. By discovering what I ate (which was <u>not</u> the same as what I thought I ate) I got back in control.

---

42   www.scottishslimmers.com

Metabolic Typing

The big change I made was to cut back on carbohydrate. My portion of breakfast cereal was reduced to a quarter, my bread consumption went down to less than half and the amount of potato, rice or pasta I had with evening meals was slashed. On the other hand, I ate more meat and fish. I was less hungry, had loads more energy and could get into my trousers again.

My new style of eating really suited me and 5 years later I still feel great. However, it may not suit you. Now I have studied metabolic typing, I realise that we're all different. A worthwhile investment in your health (see chapter 11) is to find out about your body chemistry.

The government-advised food pyramid or eat-well plate, with its emphasis on lots of starchy food and minimal fat is only right for a fraction of the population and could be damaging to the health of the others, as it was for me. There's a lot of confusing and conflicting advice these days so it's worth finding out what's best for you.

Fat vs Sugar

In recent years, fat has been treated as public enemy number one. There's a general belief that eating fat causes people to put on weight. Consequently, low-fat food products are labelled as healthy, regardless of what else they contain. But we actually eat less fat now than 50 years ago[43] so what is causing our ever-expanding waistlines?

Personally I think that the number one culprit is processed food almost all of which contains sugar (sometimes hidden under different

---

43   www.personal-nutrition.co.uk

names).   Ready meals, fizzy drinks and 'recreational food' (chocolate bars, crisps, biscuits and cakes) could be the main causes of the current obesity and diabetes epidemics.

Eat real food

The only way to lose weight and improve your health is quite simply to change the way you eat. Britain now has the worst diet in Europe. Following the lead of our American cousins (who eat 90% processed food)[44], cooking from scratch has gone out of fashion and ready meals are the norm. Buying simple, natural foods will save you money and you'll get higher quality. You can't do better than freshly prepared real food.

If you're trying to change your habits to improve your health, the best way to discipline your eating is in your shopping.

---

44   www.mercola.com

Once food is in the house it will be eaten however bad it is for you. Cut out the pre-prepared food, drink and take-aways. These often lack vital vitamins, minerals and fibre. Go back to basics and cook yourself good nutritious meals from fresh ingredients. Eat meat, fish and lots of fruit and veg.

A really good breakfast gets your metabolism going. Experiment and find out what makes you feel best. Never make do with coffee and a croissant which will leave you feeling hungry and irritable; you'll soon be reaching for the biscuit tin. Cereal bars might be quick and easy but they too are processed, recreational food. Their ingredients vary widely so always check the labels, but most have little nutritional value and they're not cheap.

You can save a lot of money by making your own lunches too. Snack on fruit mid-morning, drink water and have salad for lunch with meat, fish, egg or cheese (if you work, take it in a sealed container). It will boost your health and cost less than buying chocolate bars, crisps, sandwiches and drinks from vending machines or shops.

Toxins

Even low calorie food and drink can put weight on you. Generally these are loaded with chemicals such as sweeteners, colourings, flavourings and preservatives. Your system, already stressed by the modern diet, cannot process and eliminate all of these substances. As an emergency measure, your body is able to protect you from this toxic waste by storing it safely out of the way in fat cells.

Get into the habit of reading labels on the food you buy. A fruit yoghurt for example, should contain yoghurt, fruit and perhaps a little sugar, nothing else.

Slow down

Another characteristic of today's lifestyle is that everything has to be instant. We're so impatient, wanting everything NOW. This too pushes us towards convenience food. But in truth, cooking doesn't have to take long. Your eating habits have a direct effect on your health and your mood. If feeling good matters to you, make time to take care of yourself.

> He who enjoys good health is rich, though he knows it not.[45]

---

45   Italian proverb.

Exercise

A bit of exercise will switch your body from fat storing mode to fat burning mode. Even 20 minutes can give benefits for several hours. Richard Simmons[46], an inspirational American trainer who runs exercise classes for the seriously overweight, knows how important this is and is great at getting people moving. Exercising need not cost a lot. Just a brisk walk will do you good. I like to go out every lunchtime and find that in the afternoon I feel fresher and more alert.

---

46   www.richardsimmons.com

Gym membership costs vary around the country and can be huge but there are lots of cheap alternatives:

- use videos to exercise in privacy
- borrow books/DVDs from the library
- go to local night classes
- buy dumb-bells and work out at home
- dance; it's great exercise and lots of fun

Slim and fit

So save yourself a few £s while you shed the lbs. Buy fresh food and spend a little time in the kitchen preparing yourself healthy, low cost meals. Increase your energy and tone up by exercising your body in a way you really enjoy. You'll soon be looking and feeling great.

13 GAMBLING

If you're going to survive, defending yourself against predators is vital. Remember, everyone wants your money. Even if you can walk along the cliff edge yourself, there are perils to trip you up and Sirens to lure you into danger. Walking into a gambling den is like walking into a lion's den. Are you ready to protect yourself or will you be devoured?

As pastimes go, few have so much style, tension and excitement as gambling, or such an addictive quality. It's your money and next time, you could win.

In the USA, casinos are a $billion industry. They provide fabulously exotic interiors and free drinks to entice you in. The staff are immaculate and obliging. They want you to feel comfortable and have a good time. We haven't reached such heights of plush extravagance in the UK, but we're catching on fast. All of us are familiar with the lottery and slot machines in pubs. Every town has its betting shops. On-line gambling websites are popping up all the time with email pinging into your in-box every day inviting you to join the games. The onslaught is growing at an alarming rate. Even Bingo has spiced up its image.

The operators tap into your hopes and dreams and try to make you believe that they will make them come true. The glamorous image is reinforced on TV and in films. James Bond is often seen in casinos keeping his cool under pressure. It all adds to the appeal.

Actually the buzz is so great that there is also danger. Gambling can be addictive. If you get hooked you can get into a lot of trouble very quickly. The more you lose, the more you wish your luck would change, so you try again and again in the hope that you'll recover your losses. If that's you, get help. Don't hide your problem until you've lost everything that matters in your life. There are lots of organisations and charities (such as Gamblers Anonymous[47] and GamCare[48]) that offer support.

So can you win? Occasionally perhaps. In the long run, probably not. Over a hundred years ago the black cloth covered the gaming table at Monte Carlo in Monaco. The 'man who broke the bank at Monte Carlo' was the con man Charles Wells who later spent several years in jail for fraud and died poor.[49]

---

47   www.gamblersanonymous.org.uk
48   www.GamCare.org.uk
49
http://en.wikipedia.org/wiki/Charles_Wells_(gambler)

Recognise that the reason why so many people operate casinos, internet gambling sites, betting shops and arcades is because the owners make lots of money out of it - OUR MONEY. I used to rent a house from a man who owned a betting shop. He had gold fittings in his bathroom worth more than the house we lived in!

So don't be seduced by promises of fun and fortune. The odds are very carefully calculated so it's a mathematical fact that you're unlikely to be the one who gets rich. The people doing the gambling almost always lose.

OK, people do win sometimes and very occasionally, win handsomely. This is the Sirens' lure, splashed across all the promotional material, which leads so many to ruin. If you gamble often, even the occasional win is soon swallowed up among the losses.

Awareness will get you back in control. As we've seen in other chapters, knowledge is power. Keep a record of how much you put in and how much you get back. You may quickly discover that the rate of interest is large and negative. Betting is not an investment on which you can expect to receive a return.

Gambling should be viewed as a form of entertainment that you pay for, much the same as going to the cinema or a football match. The amount you bet is the price of the activity of gambling. It's the amount of money you're prepared to part with, probably for ever, to take part in the experience.

Perhaps the super rich are the only ones who have the wealth to keep playing, although even they sometimes come to ruin and lose vast fortunes. For the rest of us on a finite budget, whether large or small, can we really afford it?

Once you find out what it's really costing you, only you can judge whether the pleasure you get is worth the price you pay. We all have things we are prepared to pay for: shoes, computer games, sports, meals out.... Is gambling a hobby you can afford and enjoy with your eyes open? Or is it a non-essential expense, a target to be eliminated in the battle to end skintness?

14 NECESSARY NASTY BITS

Having enjoyed thinking about shopping and children, here are three somewhat dry topics to consider. They may lack glamour but they're important and you need to deal with them.

Pensions

If you're young and skint you may not like the idea of investing any of your precious cash in a pension. But do you really want to end up old and skint? Thought not.

It's never too early to start putting money into a pension or other form of long term savings or investment plan. If you don't like the idea, start small, but do start. Never be tempted to cash in this money when you run low on ready cash. It's strictly hands off. Most long term investments also carry heavy penalties for early surrender.

A single life pension is fine if you're single but if you're married you'll want a pension that pays out to your spouse if you die. There are many products available and they change often. A financial adviser will help you decide on the best scheme for your personal circumstances.

Your Will

A will is not something that helps your financial situation but is invaluable to your nearest and dearest if the worst were to happen. Dying intestate (without a will) causes huge problems because lawyers might have to trace all your relatives and divide your estate between them. The work involved in doing this uses a chunk of your life's savings and the remainder may not end up where you would wish.

It's very easy to draw up a simple will. A solicitor can advise you[50], there are internet services, or pick up a do-it-yourself 'will pack' at the Post Office or stationers.

---

50   The Society of Will Writers. www.willwriters.com

Insurance

What a total waste of money insurance is - until you suffer the calamity it would have protected you against!

You can insure against almost anything. Whether you want to is a decision based on the likelihood of need. The most important things to insure are:

- Your car (required by law)
- Your home building (for rented properties the landlord may cover this - but do check)
- Your home contents

If you have dependants it is advisable to insure:

- Your life

You may also consider:

- Some form of income protection or mortgage payment protection
- Health insurance or critical illness cover (these can be expensive and you need to check carefully what's included in the cover)

Get financial advice; there are hundreds of products to choose from. You might not enjoy thinking about such gloomy disasters but it's a big bad world and you won't be lucky all the time. If something happens to you, it will be a big relief to know that you had it covered.

15 FROM SKINT TO SURVIVOR

You've completed your survival course. Knowing that you won't fall or be knocked down to the rocks of financial ruin, you can walk along the top of the cliff with confidence.

You've always known how tough the world is. As you walk the cliff-top path of life's ups and downs, you might struggle again. But next time you'll reach for the head torch, knowing that increasing your awareness puts you back in control. You can make a map showing where you are and where you want to go.

Understanding what's really important in your life enables you to prioritise. Using cash helps keep your journey within your limits, like a fence to stop you falling off the edge.

You have some savings put away to catch you like an emergency safety rope if needed.

You know all about how many people want your money. You recognise that advertisers are trying to lure you into buying things you don't need by making you dissatisfied with the life you have. With your blinkers and ear defenders on, you move fast to dodge those predators and avoid falling victim to their wiles. By saving first and buying later, no shark will bite a chunk out of you through interest on credit or debt.

If you have children, you're able to provide for them, teach them about money and lead them confidently in life's expedition.

You know you can stay in control, so now relax, see how good life is and enjoy. May you always survive.

RESOURCES

General advice and support

Citizens' Advice Bureau

www.citizensadvice.org.uk

Financial Services Authority

www.moneymadeclear.fsa.gov.uk

0300 500 5000

Direct Gov (includes information on money,

tax and benefits)

www.direct.gov.uk

Shelter (housing and homelessness charity)

www.shelter.org.uk

Consumer Credit Counselling Service (CCCS)

www.cccs.co.uk

0800 138 1111

Credit Action (money education charity)

www.creditaction.org.uk

0207 380 3390

National Debtline (free confidential and
independent advice)

www.nationaldebtline.co.uk

0808 808 4000

The Society of Will Writers

www.willwriters.com

01522 68 78 88

Gamblers Anonymous (fellowship of men and
women who meet to overcome their
compulsive gambling)

www.gamblersanonymous.org.uk

GamCare (gambling counselling charity)

www.gamcare.org.uk

0845 6000 133

The Samaritans (confidential emotional
support service)
www.samaritans.org
08457 90 90 90

Environmental and Waste Reduction
The Freecycle Network (not for profit
movement promoting gifting to reduce waste)
www.freecycle.org.uk

The Furniture Re-Use Network
www.frn.org.uk
0117 954 3571

Recycling information
www.recyclenow.com

Carplus (charity promoting responsible car
use)
www.carplus.org.uk
0113 234 9299

Clean Green Cars (environmentally friendly cars and driving)
www.cleangreencars.co.uk

The Love Food Hate Waste campaign raising awareness of the need to reduce food waste
www.lovefoodhatewaste.com
0808 1002040

Other
Personal Nutrition (nutrition and metabolic typing)
www.personal-nutrition.co.uk

Colour analysis
www.ColourMeBeautiful.co.uk
020 7627 5211

Alexander Technique
www.stat.co.uk

Books

Libraries have books for reference and loan as well as DVD hire and computers for use.

Almost anything by Alvin Hall. For example, Money for Life, Alvin Hall, Hodder & Stoughton, 2000
ISBN: 0-340-79321-X

How to Change you Life in 7 Steps, John Bird, Vermillion, 2007
ISBN: 0091907039

The Money Secret, Rob Parsons, Hodder and Stoughton, 2005
ISBN: 978-0340862773

Happiness Now, Robert Holding, Hodder & Stoughton, 1998
ISBN: 0-340-71308-9

Money, Sex and Power, Richard J Foster,
Hodder & Stoughton, 1987
ISBN: 978-0340413937

The 7 Habit of Highly Effective People,
Stephen R. Covey, Simon & Schuster UK Ltd,
2004
ISBN: 978-0684858395

Taming the Paper Tiger, Barbara Hemphill,
Times Books, 1997
ISBN: 978-0812928365

Touch Typing in 10 Hours, Ann Dobson, How
to Books Ltd, 2002
ISBN: 1-85703-827-4

Eat that Frog, Brian Tracey, Berrett-Koehler
Publishers Inc , 2002
ISBN: 978-1576751985

Freedom Flight, Lanny Bassham, Mental
Management Systems, 2008
ISBN: 978-1-934324-18-9

What not to Wear, Trinny Woodall and
Susannah Constantine, Weidenfeld & Nicolson,
2003
ISBN: 1-841-88234-8

Building Self-Esteem, A Practical Guide to
Growing in Confidence, Sue Atkinson, Lion,
2001
ISBN: 0 7459 31138

Living Simply, Fiona Castle and Jan
Greenough, Kingsway Communications Ltd,
2006
ISBN: 978-1-842912-52-2

The Life you can Save, Peter Singer, Picador, 2009

ISBN: 978-0330454582